AWFUL GREEN STUFF

AND

THE NAKEDNESS OF TREES

The Way It Used to Be, the Way It Is

*To Char
with great admiration

Harriette Ferriger-Leidich*

November, 2003

AWFUL GREEN STUFF

AND

THE NAKEDNESS OF TREES

The Way It Used to Be, the Way It Is

Harriette Lerrigo-Leidich

Rutledge Books, Inc.

Danbury, CT

ALL RIGHTS RESERVED
Rutledge Books, Inc.
107 Mill Plain Road, Danbury, CT 06811
1-800-278-8533
www.rutledgebooks.com

Manufactured in the United States of America

Cataloging in Publication Data
Lerrigo-Leidich, Harriette

    Awful Green Stuff and The Nakedness of Trees: The Way It
      Used to Be, the Way It Is

    ISBN:1-58244-135-9

    1. Collection of Articles. 2. Bennington Banner

Library of Congress Catalog Card Number: 00-111253

INTRODUCTION

In January 1999, to my amazement and to others' amusement, I again became a newspaper columnist. I was 86 years old at the time. It was a return to a job I had first done when I was 14 years old.

My first column as a teenager—written for my father's country newspaper in Nebraska—reported on runaway horses, watermelon trucks, the advent of a new device called a radio, and the banker's new car, significant because it had roll-down windows! My first column as an octogenarian reflected on the importance of Christmas cards.

Actually my first piece for the *Bennington Banner*, which has been publishing my column, was about a birthday party for a 90-year-old friend who is a well-known and widely traveled anthropologist. That article, a tribute to my friend's illustrious career, was printed in the "Letters to the Editor" section. Seeing my words in print inspired me. I asked the editor if she would consider a column on my experiences from 80-plus years of living, and suggested the title "Once Upon A Time." The editor chose to call my stories "Senior Moments."

Janice Campbell

My occasional columns appeared on the Monday editorial page. My older friends shared their appreciation for the recollections of the way life used to be. My younger friends thanked me for sharing a time and perspective they had not previously known. I was further inspired, and began cranking out more and more columns. Some weeks the *Banner* published as many as three columns. So my mornings always begin with a trip to my mailbox to pick up the day's paper and see if yet another "Senior Moment" has reached readers.

I want to thank my sons for their encouragement and help in this endeavor. My older son, Charles Lerrigo, an ordained Methodist minister and a journalist in California, encouraged me to pull these columns together in a book and has helped with some editing. My younger son, George Lerrigo, a French teacher for 30 years who lives a short stroll through the woods, has been my sounding board and supporter. George also understands computers, which I do not, and he has helped make this book electronically possible.

Thanks to Janice Campbell, a Bennington artist, for the sketch of me at my typewriter and Ruth Randall, also an artist friend for the naked tree drawing. Thanks to Joe Karius, publisher of the *Bennington Banner,* for the legal permission to share these columns with you, to Robin Smith, managing editor of the *Banner,* and to my special friend Betty Benedict who has quietly applauded my efforts.

Most of these columns are about another time, years ago. They are about cars and strange fruits and sunflowers and cabbages, and about the little things of life in a time that might otherwise be forgotten. Other stories are reflections on how today's world looks to someone who has been around for close to 90 years.

I hope you enjoy them.

— Harriette Lerrigo-Leidich
North Bennington, Vermont 2000

Awful Green Stuff

While shopping for groceries the other day I saw these rather large, fine-looking avocados. I'm fond of this tropical American fruit that is cultivated in California and the southern United States. In some places, they are called alligator pears. But $1.59 apiece? Wow!

I got my introduction to avocados back in 1926. My father had gone to California to visit his retired parents. Before leaving our little Nebraska town, he bought a large luggage trunk. My mother wondered why he needed such a trunk. He didn't take much clothing. And he shipped the trunk ahead of him, empty.

My father took a portable typewriter with him as he got on the train out of Omaha to go to the "land of the sun." He planned to contribute a travelogue piece each day and send them back from railroad stops along the way. This was his first trip to California.

I don't remember who was left in charge of the little country newspaper my father edited, but I think my older brother, local correspondents, and the whole family pitched in to put out the weekly editions. I had a little column called "This 'n That" which filled some of the space.

When my father's vacation was over, he headed home. But the mysterious trunk arrived before he did. It was so heavy. When we opened it, we found a trunkful of California oranges and grapefruit. This was a great treat in 1926. Fresh fruit wasn't that plentiful and was very expensive in the Midwest.

Among the citrus, however, was a carefully wrapped package. The family gathered around as my mother opened it. Inside were three leathery looking, greenish-black ovals. We didn't know what they were. Mother said we'd have to cut one open. Father wouldn't have sent it back if it weren't edible, she reasoned.

She peeled away the leathery skin. Inside was some awful greenish pulp. "It must be spoiled," my mother said. Then, thinking that the green stuff might be covering something better inside, she pared away the pulp to find a very hard seed or nut.

This, we all decided, must be the edible part. But we couldn't crack it open. In disgust, we gave up and threw it away. Maybe the next one would reveal the treat our father had planned. Mother peeled another oval.

The same thing. We found the same greenish pulp and impossibly hard nut. Maybe the treat had gotten spoiled on its trip to Nebraska, we thought, as we cut up the third one and threw the whole lot out.

You can imagine my father's chagrin when he returned home several days later and discovered that we had tossed out a prize edible which was then being grown in the "land of the sun." You can also imagine the embarrassment and humiliation my mother and we siblings felt when we learned that this very choice fruit would have made an excellent addition to our salads.

Anyway, things went back to normal in our home. We children had a double exposure to Vitamin C with all the citrus, but we remained a little red-faced as we learned that the green pulp doesn't necessarily mean a fruit is rotten. And we had to wait until later in life to discover the delight of avocados.

A LIFETIME OF PLASTIC WRAP

A funny thing happened to me at the beginning of the week. I had a call from a veterans' organization with a fast-talking member on the horn. He started out with a mile-a-minute spiel, obviously well rehearsed. I explained I have a hearing impairment and asked him to slow down. He slowed down a little. But with the background noise of the other salesmen spurring him on, he soon returned to his high-speed motormouthing.

The telemarketer first tried to interest me in light bulbs that last seven years. I told him that at the age of 86 I wasn't interested because I didn't think I'd be needing light bulbs that long. He was undeterred. The next item in his spiel was a product for taking odors out of refrigerators. Those smells are often caused by dibs and dabs of leftovers that old people seem to think will be used for some future meal. That was appealing, but I didn't think my refrigerator smelled bad enough to buy his product.

Then my friendly "veteran" added a nice lilt to his voice as he ballyhooed a thousand-foot roll of plastic wrap. I told him I thought his product was the pits! I've fought many battles with ordinary Saran-type wraps, and I don't think a decade's supply of plastic wrap is a necessity for an octogenarian.

He slowed down a bit and sounded a little disappointed. So I jokingly asked if he had anything else he wanted to try and sell me. "Yeah," he said. "How about T-shirts?" Well. That was another loser. I'm hobbling around in my Mother Hubbards and my body is not shaped for loose T-shirts.

I could have hung up on the guy, but I stayed on the line to hear his repertoire of wares. I'm glad I did. When someone is trying to sell me something that will "last a lifetime" (so to speak) I'm out of it. I just won't be around long enough to enjoy that lasting quality. Despite my disinterest the young man (or maybe he was a happy, older "veteran") did say that with my voice and humor he didn't think I would be listed in the obituaries any time soon. That felt good. There are some compensations to being a senior.

I just hope his next customer was a younger person.

ALL THE NEWS FIT TO PRINT

I recently confided in a friend that when I was 14 years old, I became a columnist for the country newspaper my father owned. I also confessed there were only 350 souls in that long-ago Nebraska town.

"What," my friend wanted to know, "was there to report on in such a small berg?" Well . . .

There was activity on the main drag last week when a flatbed truck with sideboards loaded with watermelons from the Missouri river bottom land pulled up near the town pump. They were selling—for fifty cents—the most delicious watermelons. The vendor was always willing to "plug" (cut a three-cornered piece out of the melon) to see if it was ripe enough for the buyer. Word spread that the watermelon truck was in town, and before the day ended the melons were all sold. . . .

Henry Cawthorn's team of horses ran away when they shied at a car that was backfiring. . . . Art Blankel doesn't have a tin awning over his storefront, but there are two trees in front. He's built a plank seat there where people can rest in the shade on their trips to town. . . .

The county commissioner was informed of a loose plank that rattled as you crossed the bridge over Shaw Creek; it was expected that it would soon be fixed by the road crew. . . . Peach season has begun. Annie McArdle reports that she has canned 54 quarts and stored them in the cellar for later use. . . .

Chauncey Furst drove his spring wagon into town with a bumper crop of tomatoes. They were quickly bought up for canning by house-wives. Word of mouth spreads fast when fresh food comes to town. . . .

A pink-and-blue shower was held for the young couple who were married last year. . . . Banker John Stall is driving around town in his new Ford sedan. It has roll-down windows. . . . Herman Bruhn, who had a stroke several months ago, was seen walking in front of his home with his wife. He was using a cane. . . .

The Searchlight Study Club took up the subject of Shakespeare's Sonnets at their last meeting. . . . The Department of Agriculture's 4-H Clubs are offering instruction in farming and home economics. The 4-H Uneeda Cooking Club had as their project this week the baking of gems, which are a kind of muffin. . . . The 4-H Club will go on an overnight camping trip to Talmage where they will learn more about Head, Heart, Health and Hands. . . .

The Boy Scout troop of seven young men had an overnight camp out at Sleepy Hollow Campground. . . . Rose Zimmerman took the honors for the prettiest flowers in her garden; her dahlias are big and beautiful. . . . A new telephone operator is being trained at the local switchboard. She will help out when the owner is away from the exchange. . . . The Missouri Pacific Railroad has a crew of gandy dancers working on the main track between our town and Omaha. They are staying in boxcars along the siding. . . . A seedling fir tree has been planted in the little park just off Main Street near the town pump. Also, a small stone bench has been placed nearby. . . .

A crew of masons has arrived to rebuild the store that burned a few months ago. . . . One of the more affluent families has had a large Philco cabinet radio delivered to their home. . . . Farmer Zack Gerson has pur-chased a new threshing machine and will go on the circuit with it next summer when the grain is ripe. . . . The Ladies Aid has set up frames in the back parlor of the Congregational church and are making a quilt for the daughter of the pharmacist, whose engagement has just been announced. The couple will be married next month. . . .

The Home Missionary Society is wrapping bandages for the overseas missions fields. . . . Graham and Sarah James have sold their 360-acre farm and are moving into town. They have bought the house of Matilda Matson, who passed away recently. . . .

The old boardwalk between the ice cream parlor and the harness shop has been ripped up and a new concrete sidewalk is in place. . . . The Ladies Aid will serve pot roast, mashed potatoes and gravy, peas and carrots, and apple pie on the 29th. . . .

That's what I remember happened in my little town when I was a 14-year-old columnist.

CHRISTMAS CONNECTIONS

The Twelve Days of Christmas end January 6. That's the day I take down my tree and put the decorations away for another year. It's also the day I sort my Christmas cards.

I'm a confirmed card sender. Having lived in ten states, I've picked up quite a list of friends and don't want to lose touch with them. This year I mailed 111 cards. I received 83 in return.

After sorting the cards and checking for proper addresses, I check off the "no shows." Some may have died. Others may consider it too much effort to send a card. The cost of stamps keeps going up, too.

For me, though, Christmas cards are a way of keeping in touch. Some of my cards contained letters, pictures of children, pictures of grandchildren, and sometimes pictures of great-grand-children. Two of my contemporaries were brave enough to send their own photos. (I would never do that at my age.) One dear friend included a poem that had won a prize.

Some cards bring sadness. There was one reporting on a heart bypass. Another friend, who remembers my giving her a pearl bracelet 30 years ago, tells me her heart is weakened.

I have three sisters older than I. One talked about having all her Christmas preparations done, except for making popcorn balls. Popcorn balls! For whom, I wonder. She lives alone. Her children are long gone from the nest. But she's always made pop-corn balls, and I guess she needs to keep up the practice.

More often, the cards bring good news. The most heartening and courageous message this year came from a 77-year-old friend who had just earned her baccalaureate. I'm sure she will go on enriching humanity in her own lovely way. Another courageous friend who lost a leg from diabetes told how she manages her life. She had gone traipsing off to Europe and Asia with me when there was nothing else to do.

A nephew wrote glowingly about his parents' 60th wedding anniversary. The family hired a limo and drove into Denver for a dinner celebration. On the return trip the youngsters insisted on stopping for ice cream so they could give their orders through the limo's sunroof. Seeing his 82-year-old parents walking through the woods on a hunting trip almost made him believe in immortality, he wrote.

One nice note included a picture of a young man. I couldn't believe the young face staring back at me is the one I used to sit on the floor and play blocks with. I couldn't do that now with my arthritic knees, but it seems like it was just a short time ago.

One friend always sends a picture of an old church. She was late this year because she and three friends had just returned from a cruise on the *Queen Elizabeth II*. Last year, her church picture showed a mid-Atlantic structure built in 1731. The cost of the church was 140,000 pounds of tobacco. Great-great-great-grandfather Longfellow was baptized in that church more than 200 years ago, she reported.

Another late message came from a nephew and niece who confessed they were so busy they didn't get to the task on time. They called their message an Epiphany Epistle. At first, I had a problem figuring out who wrote the letter. The writer stated that he guessed "the job of getting the letter out was up to Blossom, Graybelle and me to finish." The tongue-in-cheek comment made sense after I learned that Blossom and Graybelle were the family cats, and that the writer was the father. He spoke of the gentle tenor voice of one of his sons that brought warmth and inspiration into their home. When he wrote that his wife was the "real heart of the family," I knew there was love, devotion, and caring in that marriage.

Another 80-year-old friend wrote that she had decided Tibet would be her next destination. The Himalayas would not be for me; the Green Mountains of Vermont are more my speed, but I am inspired by the enormous enthusiasm my friend brings to her concentration on Asian travel.

One delightful card was signed by members of a former church group. Another friend mailed a second card after she got my new Vermont address. She wanted to "keep in touch," she emphasized. Even the mail carrier and the newspaper delivery person sent a card.

As I put away these Christmas mementos I experienced a sense of elation and connection. Another year has passed. I know my friends and relatives are still out there, and care enough to send a message. And to those who profane Christmas cards as "unnecessary," I say they are silly old Scrooges!

CLICK, CLICK, CLICK . . .

Some time ago the publisher of the *Bennington Banner*, our local paper, wrote how the paper would have to replace its computers to deal with the Y2K problem. That set me thinking about my reaction to computers.

When I first walked into the *Banner* newsroom, I went into culture shock. There was no smell of printer's ink or "hot type." The rumble of the printing presses that I remember from my youth and middle age was not there. Just a steady click, click, click of electric keyboards and eyes fixed on computer screens. I was amazed at how computerized newspapers have become.

I have a computer. Some good friends were replacing theirs to get one that did color and they offered me their old one. They even helped me create a niche in my den and installed the computer. I thought it would be great to go click, click, click with the rest of the world. My friends spent hours with me. They wrote out simple directions so I wouldn't have to study a manual. Then they left me to my own devices.

I tried and tried. It worked just fine while my friends were there. But the moment they left, nothing went smoothly. When I read that Bill Gates's two-year-old daughter "gets a kick" out of the software she's using to learn the alphabet, I almost cried. I just can't seem to get the hang of it. Is it possible comprehension is not possible at my age? I feel utterly stupid that I cannot grasp the techniques youngsters seem to pick up so readily in grade school.

Maybe I need a newer model. That's possible. When the publisher wrote of their computers, he defined an "old computer" as one that was made before today's lunch. But maybe it's possible I have a mental block.

Then again, I feel a little better when I talk to my contemporaries. When I confess that I have a computer I can't use, they nod understandingly. They whisper to me; they don't understand computers either.

* * * * *

Since the above column appeared in the *Banner*, I've gotten a lot of flack about my computer illiteracy. I've had people call and offer to come by and help me get computer smart. They had so many good reasons for my ineptitudes being reversed that I am almost afraid to mention the word "computer" to anyone. Maybe I should just say I crashed my computer. I think that's the vernacular.

But I guess I've had my 15 minutes of fame. I'm still adamant about not wanting to learn how to operate a computer—even the very latest model. I just can't think on a computer.

The way I put words together is very old-fashioned. Writers used to peck out their stories on manual typewriters and then go over them with a blue pencil until they had it right. There is one noted reporter who still uses a manual machine. I'm a modern Millie compared to him; my typewriters of recent years have all been electrics.

So I cheered and felt vindicated when I read that the *New Yorker* is moving its offices to new quarters in Times Square. That magazine has always published significant writers like E.B. White, Dorothy Parker, James Baldwin, J.D. Salinger (and yes, my late brother-in-law James Reid Parker). Its new office will be housed in a chrome-and-glass lipstick tube of an office building. What made me cheer was that staff members were nostalgic and nervous at the move. Deborah Garrison is one of those editors. She's been at all the other locations where the *New Yorker* was published. She lamented the loss of her "panoramic views of the New York City Public Library and the lush greenery of Bryant Park." And she said she would take along her Correcting Selectric III typewriter, circa 1975. She said she'd also take with her carbon paper and pink routing slips.

Bless Ms. Garrison's heart! A gal after my own heart. She is like me—or I am like her—in that I hate to let old things pass into oblivion or go to the junk heap. If she as a *New Yorker* editor can hang onto her 1975 typewriter, then I don't feel ashamed at putting my words on paper with an electric typewriter, circa 1985!

JANE'S DAY

Sunday, August 2, 1998, was unquestionably and totally "Jane's Day" at North Bennington's Park-McCullough Mansion. An open-air tent was set up on the front lawn to accommodate the more than 500 friends, relatives, and guests who came to celebrate the 90th birthday of Jane Richardson Hanks.

Jane arrived promptly at six o'clock in a vintage roadster with a rumble seat and stepped jauntily out to be greeted with many cheers. She was wearing a Jeanne Lanvin designer gown that she had purchased in Paris in 1927 for $10. She looked truly regal and smart.

Inside the tent the centerpiece was a huge ice carving of the number 90. A humongous bouquet of flowers decorated a table laden with birthday cakes. Tables full of hot and cold delectables were furnished by the guests.

Master of Ceremonies Ernie LaFontaine introduced people who spoke glowingly of Jane's accomplishments through the years. They told of her academic honors, her year in Paris as a student, the years she and her late husband and family spent in Thailand, and her continued interest in Asian studies and music.

Jane holds a doctorate in anthropology from Columbia University. Her husband, Lucien, was professor of Asian Studies at Bennington College and wrote several books before his death nine years ago. Jane and Lucien had three sons; the antics and activities of this unusual family brought laughter and cheers from those who came to honor her.

Throughout the years Jane has been an active participant in many area musical organizations. Her talent has encouraged many youngsters to take up an instrument. Music is part of her everyday life. It's not uncommon to see several cars in her driveway: musicians who come to play and practice with her for the sheer joy of creating beautiful sounds. Jane has never stopped playing the violin. Her dog was named Faust and the cats were named Mozart and Beethoven (only Mozart is still alive).

Without any hesitation or need to search for a word, Jane thanked the people and regaled them with stories of her life. She was honored two years ago in Bangkok for her work in Asian studies and presented a paper in Kunming. She has never stopped cataloguing and researching Asian studies. A book is said to be in the making.

So to Jane Hanks we say again, Happy Birthday, and may you be here when your 100th rolls around.

DOCTORING DOLLS

When I moved back to New England several years ago, I had a letter from a younger friend (in her seventies). She wondered if I would accompany her to the doll "hospital" located between Bennington and Arlington. She too had moved to be close to her children and was sorting through her possessions.

Looking through your possessions to see what you should keep or throw out is an arduous task. It's also a way to find a treasure trove forgotten for decades. When I got ready to move, I found many items that reminded me where, why, and how I had acquired them. My friend had done the same and came across two keepsakes: family dolls. She was taking them to the "hospital" to see about restoration. I happily tagged along.

We entered the "hospital" with her treasures securely wrapped in old miniature quilts. The "doctor" picked them up lovingly, turning them over and over, looking at their construction and state of preservation. They were German dolls, circa 1850, with china heads sewn onto stuffed cotton bodies. Their painted faces were sweet and serene. They wore darling clothes.

I winced as the "doctor" cut off the worn net stockings, and started to undress the doll, removing the clothes by layers. The clothing had tiny buttons, so small that old hands could hardly manage them. There were lacy borders on the pantaloons, petticoats—each different—with lace, tucks, large hems, and more tiny buttons. It reminded me of the pantywaists I wore as a child, which buttoned on the shoulders such as the doll's undergarment did.

The hands of one of the dolls had kid gloves reaching above the elbows. The gloves had deteriorated considerably, but you could still see the fingers. Her stockings were black and white and came up over the knees. Handsome leather boots, with two buttons on each boot, covered the feet of one doll; the leather was in perfect condition.

The head on one doll had sloping china shoulders sewed onto the body; this was a good feature, the "doctor" told us. Legs and arms were jointed, but the body did not bend. The body was narrow at the waist, but beneath the pantaloons were rather heavy buttocks.

The diagnosis? One doll was so well preserved it was sent home with my friend. "Hospitalization" was not needed. However, the "doctor" recommended that the doll's clothing should be washed and bleached. My friend received explicit directions on how to launder the tiny clothes without damaging the material. New stockings were prescribed, and my friend chose a brown pair, like the ones worn in Germany during the 1850s. Shoes were suggested, but the ones offered didn't seem to fit the age of the doll. It came home shoeless.

Neither of the dolls bent at the waist. Many dolls were made that way. But the "doctor" suggested that he could add a piece of cloth to the larger doll so she could sit.

My inquisitiveness got the better of my good taste. I asked what the dolls were worth. I thought maybe my friend wanted to sell them. No. She had brought them in to be made "healthy" for grandchildren and great-grandchildren.

I recalled that the dolls I grew up with were filled with sawdust. When the cloth was torn or ripped, they began to lose their shape. One of the first questions the doll "doctor" asked was "Is the doll leaking?" We discovered my friend's dolls were stuffed with cotton.

As I watched the "doctor" examine the dolls' anatomy, I thought how amazing it was that these toys were probably home-made, and that their clothes had likely been sewn from scrap material. The gauziest lace decorated sleeves and hems of all the garments. The clothes had been sewn on a machine, but the body was hand sewn with a heavy cordlike thread. Imagine thread that lasted 150 years without giving way!

How carefully children in those days cared for their toys. Maybe it was because there were so few toys. Maybe they were taught to handle them tenderly. Not like today's children. They have so many dolls, stuffed animals, etc.

I wonder how many attics, trunks, dresser drawers, sealed boxes or crates hold treasures like the ones my friend took to the doll "hospital". I also wonder how many people would treasure them as valuable family keepsakes.

The doll "hospital" showed me that very, very old dolls can be restored to "health" and pristine beauty. Also, I discovered that it's not only people hospitals where tender loving care is dispensed. There is TLC for dolls as well, and I saw it this day in a Vermont doll "hospital".

"GRANDMA ALICE"

I was surprised to read an article in a recent southern magazine telling about another Grandma Moses type of artist. She is Alice Moseley who is 89 years old and lives in Bay Saint Louis, Mississippi. She is a wit, as was our Grandma Moses of Eagle Bridge, New York, whose art hangs in the Bennington Museum in her old country schoolhouse which has been moved to the museum. Alice has won numerous awards even though she didn't take up painting until age 60 while she was taking care of her ill mother.

Alice Moseley paints in oils with a steady hand and captures life in the South. She paints every day and is quite a tourist attraction as buses stop by her little shotgun house along the Mississippi Gulf coast. Her nephew in Birmingham calls her a cross between Grandma Moses and Phyllis Diller. Her son Tim calls her a star but she admits that "she is somewhat of a ham." As she paints, she keeps her white hair under a beret because she says she doesn't have time to comb her hair anymore.

Mrs. Moseley insists that she is not a little old lady with a weekend hobby. She has won numerous awards for her art. It is a business and has a price list ranging from $5 to $5,000 for her original works.

Alice has some great remarks about aging. She says people think it's a great secret that she's working at age 89. "You have to have a reason to get up every morning. No one's promised me immortality," she says, "but I'm beginning to wonder." After her 89th birthday she started talking about the next one. "Ninety is just so much more impressive than 89," she stated. "When I stop painting you'll know my work has deteriorated, and I'll know when to stop." Her health is good despite a blood pressure problem. She turns that into a chuckle and says, "If you've got any blood pressure at all at this age it's gotta be a good sign."

When we seniors think about living beyond the promised three score and ten, it makes us think about the fears we harbor of living beyond that mythical age. Statistics point out that 46 percent of us fear declining health. Thirty-eight percent of us fear not having enough money to take care of ourselves. Only 13 percent fear losing mental faculties, but I think that's a farcical evaluation because a lot of us have that dread. Likewise only 12 percent fear dependence on others. These are AARP figures and further state that the average person wants to live to 91.

That little old lady in Mississippi and Grandma Moses had the right idea. Keep working, keep active, and perhaps you may find you have a talent that will see you through your senior years.

BIRTHDAY WISDOM AND CHEER

I just celebrated—no, observed is a better word—my 87th birthday. I marvel at how I reached this ripe old age. Life cannot be measured in years alone. I know I've spoken before about the saggy jowls, crow's-feet, wrinkles, varicose veins, arthritis twinges, the slowed step, thinning hair, reluctant muscles, faulty recall, prosthetics, unwanted pounds, and all that rigamarole; but let's face it, they are all factors in growing old-er.

To reminisce, I reread some of my last year's cards and gleaned some delightful prose used by the greeting card writers. They are so charming, delightful, and appropriate that I want to pass them on to you. They are truly words to live by:

"One must live fully, warmly and stay young at heart." "Birthdays celebrate the gift of Time." "Those who wish to sing always find a song." "Life is the music that dances through our days, nights and our years."

A crop of greeting cards came to me on this 1999 birthday. From my family came the most special ones. My California son sent a wacky card with a framed likeness of my engagement picture which appeared in the Topeka, Kansas, *Daily Capital* in 1935. (How I wish I looked like that now.) The inside was printed with this comment, "Now in its 87th smash year—the Harriette show." Amusing, touching, and respectful of my long life.

My local son and family greeted me with thoughts like "Inner contentment, relationships to cherish, taking time for yourself,

21

high expectations, dreams that come true, achievements to be proud of, year-long happiness and joy." A tall order but they concluded with the admonition that wished me "all the joy your heart can hold today and always." My granddaughter hand delivered her card with her message saying something about "spoiling her rotten for a lot of years," and ended up by treating me to a nice meal in the evening.

My stepdaughter has a special knack for finding the most beautiful sentiment on her cards. I believe they say exactly how she feels about me and they don't jibe with the "wicked stepmother" stereotype.

A friend from another state says in her card that it is my "day for dreaming; to take a quiet journey" deep into my heart and "to linger over daydreams. It is your day to let your heart speak." Another friend greets me with the message that she is now 80 and wonders how she ever got to be that old. I wonder about 87 years. A New Hampshire friend's card said, "Your birthday is a time to take life slower, to stop and savor each wonderful moment and open your heart to all the best that life can bring."

Friends and family send wonderful, meaningful messages. Of course they are helped with the witty and caring words and sentiment expressed by greeting card writers. But it wasn't only cards that spoke to me on my 87th. My favorite pink African violet decided this was the day to send out one of its delicate blooms. Even plant life knew it was my 87th.

HOORAY FOR GADGETS!

I have a new companion! It's my new portable phone. Maybe that's nothing new to you. For me, it's a much delayed gadget. Though I live in small quarters, there are times when I am 10 or 20 feet from one of my wall phones. Sometimes impatient callers don't let the phone ring long enough for me to get to it before they give up.

So for Christmas my son gave me a portable phone. I had to get help learning how to use it. I'm not very good at following directions for electronic things. I've almost mastered the techniques, but it's taken a couple of weeks to get used to carrying the phone around with me.

I wonder if I'm the last person in Vermont to have a touch-tone phone. My husband was a retiree of an AT&T subsidiary and we had perks that allowed us to buy phone equipment at cost. When we got our phones, touch-tone dialing was not yet common. We got the table-top variety, with long cords so we could carry them around.

I'm still a bit embarrassed when I call an 800 number for information and am told to "Press 1 if . . . " and "Touch 2 if . . . " and "If not, please hold until someone can take your call." Sometimes I wait long minutes for a real person to pick up on the other end.

But this year, I say hooray for gadgets. I'm getting used to my cordless, touch-tone phone, and I give thanks to the company that

made it so I can save a lot of steps and get calls I might otherwise
have missed.

THE HUDSON SUPER SIX

In 1916, a family of four piled into their big Hudson Super Six and set out for California. Driving all but 40 miles of the distance was a young woman who was a mere four feet 10 inches tall with her shoes on. The trip took 15 days, including stops to visit friends along the way.

The family left Griswold, Iowa (my birthplace), on the Striped Pole Road. It took them as far as Omaha, which picked up the road to Fairmont, Nebraska, where they connected with the Blue Ball Route. It took them to McPherson, Kansas, where they hit the Santa Fe Trail—which they followed to their destination in Los Angeles.

Nowhere on the entire trip did they find a place they could not have passed another car with the exception of one turn, on a mountain pass, where they had to back the car up to get around a pile of rocks. On both sides of that pass the American Automobile Association had men stationed who let cars through, one at a time.

When the family arrived in Los Angeles, news of the drive reached the ears of Hudson dealers, and the young woman was besieged by reporters. She had become the second woman driver to cross the mountains into California. Other women who made the trip had specially prepared cars and support teams. The automobile of my story was a year old at the time of the journey; nothing special had been done to it.

The Hudson Super Six was a handsome black touring car with leather upholstery. In between the front and rear seats were little jump seats, favorite spots for us children who were given a ride. The car carried two big spare tires, one mounted on each of the side running boards. The trunk on the rear didn't hold much luggage, but it did have the vulcanizing equipment necessary to fix flat tires. Thankfully, there was only one flat on the historic trip to California, a puncture just outside of Omaha.

I loved those old touring cars. We had a Maxwell that only my father drove. When it rained the side curtains had to be brought out from under the backseat and snapped into place. It was a great sensation, riding along and feeling the wind in my face. I recall trips where the vulcanizing equipment was brought out to fix a flat. Some cars had cranks but the Hudson Super Six had a self-starter.

This is a special story because that little mite of a woman was my Aunt Ethel. I can see her sitting on a raised cushion steering that long car. The family liked California and in 1919 the trip was made again across the mountains. Passengers this time—with my aunt driving—were her parents and two brothers just returned from the war. My aunt always wore a little dust cap and I still have a vision of her driving down the road in that big touring car.

DESPERATELY SEEKING PORTION CONTROL

I did it again! I vowed I would not eat out again and have to carry half my entree home in a doggie bag. But I did just that last weekend and I'm furious at my lack of restraint. I promise myself not to eat out again until I can find a place where they recognize senior appetites.

There are lots of things I could complain about when I go out. I want to tell the chef that the steak isn't quite cooked to order, that the fish is overdone, and that the salad bar has such wimpy greens and ordinary condiments that I almost want to pass it by. The waitress comes by and asks "how is everything?" I suspect an honest answer doesn't get back to the chef. He's too busy with his big serving spoon and ladle, meat fork, and over-cooked veggies!

It's the size of the servings that disturbs me. Big eaters and big portions must be a New England phenomenon. I was in an A-one café in New Hampshire and complained about the huge size of my serving. The waitress told me most customers want a lot of food. There were no exceptions, and I had to take a doggie bag from there, too.

So what does one do? I could stay home and cook my own meals. Or I could grin and bear it. I suggest that if the chef isn't too busy he might case the crowd and see who his customers are. If it's a place seniors flock to and he sees a lot of gray heads, he should take note and dish accordingly.

It isn't that all older folks eat like birds. We probably eat sensibly at home and going out is a treat. But when we get the "more is better" treatment, we may wish we'd stayed at home.

Surely there's a solution to this "big portions" syndrome. I've been in some restaurants where they list "petite portions" or "mini portions." Usually there's a children's menu, but it's a bit embarrassing to order from that side of the page. I don't like taking home half a meal that I probably won't eat later; things look rather unappetizing after a few days in the fridge.

Most of my senior friends feel the way I do. We'll have to seek restaurants where they cater to the more modest size of our appetites. If we can't find that sensitivity, we might just have to stay home and eat alone. I want to see an end to doggie bags.

THE HAT PEOPLE

Easter is a few days away and I'm thinking about this year's Easter bonnet. I've always been a hat person, but the beehive and teased hairdos that came into style some years ago have put hats on the back burner. Seems the only really truly hat people are Queen Elizabeth and the Queen Mother.

Hats remind me of my childhood. I remember Easter Sunday when my siblings and I went off to Sunday School, hand in hand, all wearing our little sailor hats. Lots of times the hats were hand-me-downs. Some were remodeled with a new grosgrain ribbon that hung in streamers down the back. Others were brightened up with hat dye, which gave them a glossy sheen. Italian straws were popular in those days, and could easily be renewed with hat dye.

About ten years ago I gave away many of my hats to a costume house. One of those I saved, however, was a designer's hat from New York that didn't quite make it to Europe. It was a beautiful red cloche, covered with bright red and black feathers. The label says it was an "exclusive" from a firm with shops in Paris and New York, and I had planned to wear it on my first trip to Europe 35 years ago. I'd taken it to the bon voyage party, but the more I thought about carrying it through Europe, I became concerned that it would be crushed or damaged. So I gave it to a friend at the party and asked her to keep it until I returned. She later told me my red-feathered hat made her "feel like a million dollars."

Alas, when it came time this year to choose my Easter bonnet, the once-fashionable red feathers looked sadly out of date. I wound up choosing a more modern straw version.

I've found a friend who also likes hats, and she too will wear one this Easter Sunday, and we'll sit together at church, so we won't stick out like sore thumbs.

It seems today there aren't many of us hat people left. Except, of course, the Queen and Queen Mother.

THE LOST IS FOUND

Several years ago my husband said to me, "Are you hearing everything, my dear? Maybe you should have a hearing aid. After all, I wear two and I hear everything."

With a little resentment I mentioned that I heard the buzzer on the stove, the ding of the microwave, the little clicks on the digital clock by the bed. I always heard the telephone, and I thought I was tuned in to the world.

But the more I thought about it, the more I realized I was growing older and losing some of my hearing. I took my husband's hint and had my hearing checked. The test showed I had a borderline hearing loss common to older people. That meant I should get a hearing aid.

I noticed my bridge partners twist their fingers in their ears during bidding and wondered what kind of signal that was. It was a sign they were turning up their hearing aids before the bidding began. I didn't want that little mannerism. But I joined them. Now I am an advocate for aids for all people who have a slight hearing loss.

One spring morning, though, I was having some outside work done at my little house in the woods. It was a crisp morning, but I hopped out of bed, put my hearing aid in my ear, and was off to greet the workmen.

A little later a friend came by to chat with me. I asked her to wait until I turned up my volume; she had such a soft voice. I put my finger to my ear . . . and panicked! There was no aid in my ear. I was sure I had put it in.

I looked but couldn't find it. Perhaps in emptying the waste-baskets, the aid had fallen into the trash receptacle? The truck had already picked up my trash, so my expensive prosthetic was now probably part of the town dump. And it would be a while before I could afford to buy another one.

That afternoon, I went to my DAR meeting. I never heard a bit of the program, but I talked a lot myself. Hearing-impaired people do talk a lot because they can't hear what others say, but can hear their own voice. My lack of hearing was so noticeable I compensated by over-talking.

When I got home, I continued my search for the little flesh-colored device. I turned the TV up to a high decibel, watched the news, and went to bed with a heavy heart. My hearing aid had become an important part of my body. In my evening prayers, I didn't ask to find the hearing aid. I did pray that I would be able to get along without it until I could buy a new one. I fell into a troubled sleep. There were no dreams about finding my aid.

It wasn't quite daylight when I suddenly awoke. I jumped—not too nimbly—out of bed, grabbed a flashlight, and went to the garage where the trash barrel stood. I flashed the light into it. Deep in one corner was my hearing aid.

Hallelujah! It was just lying there waiting for me to pick it up, check the battery power, and put it in my ear. The battery was still live, but not enough to emit the little squeals that aids give off when not engaged. I could afford new batteries!

My joy was boundless. I just sat down on the steps and cried. The lost was found! Those anxious hours before the rediscovery were agonizing. But my trusty little prosthetic was back, and once more I could join in a world of sounds and voices others take for granted.

A BELOVED BED

When I toured Bennington area gardens this June, an old iron bedstead that someone had used as a trellis for climbing plants caught my eye. It reminded me of the old iron bedsteads that were in vogue many, many years ago and which are now coming back into style.

It also brought to my mind a four-poster cord bed that was in my family. I had kept this relic because of its history. It was an antique, reputed to have traveled cross-country in a covered wagon with my great-grandmother Elmira Heald. She was born in 1796. It was probably the marriage bed of my grandparents Ury and John, and then was handed down to my father. I remember sleeping in the bed at my grandparents' home on an Iowa farm. We had to climb on a footstool to get into it; it was high with straw, a cotton mattress, and fluffy featherbeds.

When it came to our house, it was our sleeping frame as youngsters. It wasn't always comfortable, with its old cotton mattress and three-quarter size, but we slept in it for many years. When my parents moved to California I insisted on hauling the four-poster to Topeka, Kansas, where I lived.

It was a cord bed, with little knobs on the side and 4x4 side rails. Crisscrossed over those knobs were the ropes that supported the odd-looking spring and lumpy cotton mattress. Many times I watched my father tighten the ropes, so we could "sleep tight."

We moved from Topeka to Georgia, and later Alabama, and the bed went with us. When we moved to Massachusetts the bed was in the van. Then, as I moved into smaller quarters, it was time to begin asking who in the family wanted this heirloom.

A nephew said he wanted it and would pay to have it crated and shipped to Lawrence, Kansas, where he was on the University faculty. Knowing that my nephew John and his wife would cherish the bed, I forgot about it until one day I visited them. What a delight and vindication to see it in their guest room. They had refinished it. The simple graceful headboard still gave it character. The little nick out of one of the four posts had been filled in. It looked lovely.

I loved that old bed despite its discomfort. It was a link to the past and I didn't want to let it go for firewood. Seeing it in a home where it was treasured pleased me. The ropes had been replaced with modern springs and mattress, and now guests will sleep comfortably. No more straw or rope!

TOO LATE WE'RE SMART

The Associated Press recently focused its attention on the sweepstakes industry and the United States Senate is holding hearings that could provide federal regulations for that industry.

As I read the news release, I was awed by the many people who have been taken in by the grand offers to win millions because their name is "at the top of the list." It sickened me because I have been one of the gullible ones.

I thought it was time for my ship to come in and receive millions. I wanted to spend my few remaining years counting and spending my winnings. I don't think I've ever embraced the idea that I was going to be a winner as much as I have these past 24 months. I thought moving to New England might whirl my name to the top of the list.

How wrong could I be! Even as life slips away faster, and as each day becomes shorter, I still had hopes. The wish list I compiled on how to spend my millions was enough to snap my cranium apart.

There is method in the madness of the sweepstakes industry. They want to sell magazines and compile mailing lists for purveyors of junk. I have filled my coffee table with big glossy books. My magazine rack has become a waste paper basket. All because I've been taken in by what I didn't bargain for when I sent back my "guaranteed prize-winning envelope." I learned after the fact that I could return unopened books and articles to the sender, but I was hooked.

I began to save all the special envelopes, "personally" addressed to me, telling me I was a winner. They printed my name in big letters at the top of their announcement. I thought I was on my way to becoming a millionaire. As the stack of promises became so high that I finally decided there was no more room on my desk, I wised up and dumped the whole lot in the trash.

If sweepstakes wanted to interest people, they ought to divide those huge sums into smaller sums. Each of us would have a better chance of getting rich. Who needs a million when a couple of thousand would be welcome? There ought to be some compensation for all the books and junk I've bought.

Reputable publishing companies have exploited people's dreams. I confess with a bowed head that I'm one of those taken in by their polished palaver. Alas, as the Pennsylvania Dutch say, "Too late we become smart."

CASTOR OIL

Outside my window, brave little bulbs are busily pushing their way up through the mulch of pine needles. Inside, I'm wrestling with a winter cold. I've been fighting it for several weeks. I've tried antibiotics and bed rest, but can't shake this bug.

I can remember days when there was an antidote for almost any illness. When a member of the family become ill, out would come the castor oil. Ugh! How we hated that oily cure-all. It was administered by the tablespoonful and the spoon looked as big as a soup ladle as it neared our mouths. Even if we held our noses it always seemed hard to swallow.

If we had a chest cold or sniffles, my mother would rub camphorated hot oil on our chests, tuck a warm piece of flannel under our long nighties, and send us to bed. Perhaps we had a hot water bottle at our feet. Usually, we were much better the next morning and were sent off to school, with over-the-knee black stockings covering long underwear. There was no way to miss school if we were better.

As a child, I don't remember many visits to the doctor's office. The doctor made house calls if it was a dire emergency. We did have to go to the doctor's office for smallpox vaccinations; many of us carry the scar of those scratch-type inoculations.

Today, doctors don't make house calls. But as we grow old— or older—we seem to be in the doctor's office for so many things. We need a lot of help getting through these "golden" years. When we're ill, the years aren't golden at all. And just when we think we're feeling top-notch again, along comes another glitch. And there we go, back to the doctor's office.

My cold doesn't want to leave me. I may try some of the old home remedies I remember. But one of them won't be castor oil. I wonder if I am going to be well before those spring bulbs burst into glorious blooms.

Fan Clubs

As I write this, we're having a few days of delightfully pleasant summer weather. The leaves rustle pleasantly, giving us shade. The thermometer is comfortably in the 70s.

The newspaper reports a heat wave in other parts of the country. I can sympathize with those who are suffering from the heat. I remember how it was when I was a little girl in the Midwest. It would be so oppressive at night that we couldn't sleep upstairs. We would bring our bedding downstairs and try to fall asleep in front of open windows or doors. We made fans out of newspapers and fanned ourselves until we fell asleep.

I also remember the Japanese fans I saw as a child. In those days, Japanese imports were sleazy and made from scraps. The Japanese fans of my youth looked like two tongue depressors with colored paper glued to them. That's unlike the quality goods we have from today's Japan. But those cheap fans fascinated me, nonetheless. I could see the artistry in the way they opened into a beautiful round fan.

My Vermont son just returned from a trip to Japan, bringing me a gorgeous fan with tiny silk balls hanging from the sides. Not only was the silky material lovely, but as I waved the fan, it gave off a spicy scent that is unusual, refreshing, and pleasant.

The other day I heard a church member speak to one of the deacons saying how nice it would be if the church would provide hand fans because our sanctuary is not air-conditioned. That got me thinking how every hymn book holder of my youth had fans in it. Women, children, and even some of the men fanned themselves while the pastor droned on with his 30- to-45 minute sermons.

I remember tent revivals in the Midwest and South. They would raise the tent flaps to let the air in, and hand fans were an important accessory. Fans would be a welcome church accessory, even today. Of course, today's pastor doesn't preach more than 12 or 15 minutes—at least not in my church—so we wouldn't have to work too hard to keep cool.

THE ICEBOX

A few weeks ago I visited a Designer Showcase home in Manchester, New Hampshire. It was a fund-raising effort for the local museum, and it left me a bit breathless. The house was first built in 1860, in the Second Empire style. It has a mansard roof, dormer windows, molded cornices, and decorative brackets beneath the eaves. It was a challenge to convert that old house into a fancy, modern style.

The rooms were full of the latest gadgets and decorations. But the room that nonplussed me most was the kitchen. It was a large, bright room with long windows. The windows were dressed (we don't call them drapes or curtains anymore, but "window dressing") in bright colored fabrics. An original soapstone sink had a faucet and spray attachment that made me think it was created by Rube Goldberg. It was functional and very arty.

But as I looked around the kitchen, I couldn't see the refrigerator. What home could get along without a refrigerator? I asked the guide, and she pointed to a huge bureau with six drawers, three on each side. "That's the refrigerator," she told me. I had been looking for an upright. I wanted to pull the drawers open, just to make sure the guide wasn't fooling me.

I didn't give in to the temptation, but it reminded me of the iceboxes I grew up with. The ones I remember were made of wood and enamel. Every day, the iceman came to our house. We had a sign we were supposed to put in the window to indicate how many pounds of ice we needed.

Our iceman didn't have a truck. He had a wagon, drawn by a horse. When he arrived, we would race outside, hoping he would chip off a sliver of ice to cool our young mouths. Then he would sink his tongs into a huge block of ice on his truck, wash off the sawdust, and carry it inside to our icebox.

The icebox had three compartments. One was for the ice. There was a small space beneath that. And then, a large door the length of the box. It wasn't opened a lot. We didn't have the bottles and cans of Coke and fruit drinks we do today. Lemonade was our drink, and we chipped off pieces of the ice to cool it in a big pitcher.

Underneath the icebox was a pan. As the ice melted it dripped into the pan. If we didn't empty it regularly, we were risking an emergency. And there was always the chance that as we carried the pan, brimming with waste water, it could spill on the floor. I remember one family who bored a hole in the floor to channel the drips outside. As a child, I thought that was a very modern idea.

I remember that we children were very curious, and wanted to know how ice was made. One time we went to the icehouse. It was a large, conical building with a deep below-ground cavern. In the winter, ice was cut from a stream or lake, then packed in sawdust and stored in the cavern for the summer months. Later, ice making was automated and there were freezer lockers where people could drive up to a platform and buy 100- or 200-pound blocks of ice.

I also remember when home iceboxes were replaced by modern refrigerators. The first units I saw had a huge, round compressor on the top. We also had to defrost the units, so while the iceman didn't come anymore, we still had to contend with drips.

It's been quite a change, from ice delivered by horse-drawn wagons to a refrigerator that looks like a bureau with six drawers. I wonder what will be next.

The Poor Farm

I read recently that 6,200 Vermonters live in nursing homes. The fact set me thinking about how people handled this problem a half century ago.

I grew up in a small community, and we knew what happened when older people didn't have family to look after them or have enough money to pay for their own care. They went to the "poor farm." It was a drab and gloomy facility. As a child I hoped none of my family would ever have to go to the poor farm.

I can remember seeing a wizened, old person in a rocking chair, with a nondescript dress, her long hair twisted in an unbecoming knot, and a grim expression on her face. Maybe she was crocheting. Maybe darning a sock. Just rocking away her life. She had no loving home, no one who would care for her with easy grace and acceptance.

Many of my generation know about grandparents who lived with them. Sometimes if a grandparent, spinster aunt, or neighbor was without means to manage her life, they were taken in by family. My two sons remember a paternal grandmother whom we took in not by necessity but by choice. My children would come home from school and go right to their grandmother's room. She always had a cheery hello, a hug, and something to share with them. She might read to them, or play the piano while they sang together.

My second husband and I used to visit nursing care facilities.

It wasn't always a pretty picture. There were so many neglected oldsters who passed their days in a drift of senility. Sometimes the family visited. Most often they were left alone as wheelchair patients parked in the corridors. As we walked by, they would reach out to us to take their hand or just stop and pay some attention to them. It is the forgotten ones who tug at the heartstrings.

My husband's favorite was an 80-year-old woman (of means) who had lost both legs because of diabetes. Her spouse had passed away and there were no children. There was no place to go but to the nursing home. But each day this little bit of a woman would insist on having her hair done and some makeup applied. She tried to be pleasant and looked on the bright side of her limited existence. She was the exception, rather than the rule.

We may not have "poor farms" anymore, but we should never forget. We should never forget.

A Hot Time in the Old Town

A few years ago a disastrous firestorm swept Oakland, California, destroying hundreds of homes. I remember being very concerned. One of my sons has a home in the vicinity. He and his wife had to evacuate for a few days until the fire was under control. Fortunately, friends took them in and their house was spared.

But the Oakland firestorm reminded me of another fire. It was the night a huge flour mill burned to the ground. It was in the 1920s, and I was only a child, but old enough to join the fire brigades.

The mill caught fire in the middle of the night. The preacher's daughter got the message and ran to the church to ring the bell. A church bell ringing in the middle of the night could mean only one thing: a fire! We had no volunteer firemen. We had no fire truck. We had ourselves, and we had buckets.

My siblings and I were rousted out of bed around midnight, and told to get dressed and go down to the building that housed my father's country newspaper shop. Behind that building was a rambling wooden inn, paper-thin in construction. We could see the live coals flying all over town from the burning mill. If anything was likely to catch fire from sparks, it would be the wooden inn.

Our station was at the pump at the back of our building. We filled washtubs, barrels, boilers, buckets, kettles, and large pans. We worked that old pump so hard we were afraid it would run dry before the danger passed. All of the town's 350 inhabitants formed other bucket brigades to protect houses and businesses.

By the time we got organized, though, it was too late to save the mill. It was ablaze inside and out. Flames shot into the sky. Volunteers removed the household effects of an arthritic old woman whose home was close to the mill. They realized the heat from the mill would consume her house.

I don't remember how long the fire lasted. It seemed to me the embers flew over town for hours. Several roofs caught fire, but fire watchers caught them before they could burst into full flame.

When daylight came and the townspeople and businesses were sure there was no more danger, we were allowed to go to the fire site. The old mill was a pile of ashes. We sadly realized that an industry was gone. Flour mills were an important part of farming communities, and this one was gone.

I said that all the townsfolk came out to fight the fire. I forgot one old man who lived just a block from the mill. Little old Mr. Mosini had slept through the night. He hadn't been wakened by the shouting of the people who pumped his well dry. He didn't see the firelight; the wind was blowing away from his house. He had been spared seeing and living through the disaster that hit our little Nebraska town.

I'LL TAKE MY SURGERY
THE MODERN WAY, THANKS

I'm recovering from a little trip to our hospital's ambulatory care center. I needed another "patch up" on my body. It seems that as my days turn into months and then add up to years that I need more and more repairs to keep the old "bod" functioning.

What happened on this trip to the hospital made me recall my very first hospitalization. It was 62 years ago, and I had an ambitious appendix that grew and grew. Evidently mine was an unusual case. I had to stay in the hospital 14 days.

There was no preadmission process such as we have now. The first hospital day was spent testing, prepping, and preparing for the big "opening." The prep was done with an old-fashioned razor; it could have been a straight razor for all I know. Then I had to put on a gown, leggings, booties, and a complete head covering, all of which were cumbersome and scary. I thought I was being mummified.

They took me in, strapped my arms to the operating table (I remember that vividly!), and I knew there was no way I could back out. Anesthesia 62 years ago was done with ether. A wire-and-cloth cone was placed over my nose and the ether was poured onto the cloth. I was told to start counting to 100. I don't believe I got beyond 17 before I drifted into a state of unconsciousness. As I slipped into that state, my fate was in the hands of Dr. William Mills, a colleague of my father-in-law Dr. Charles

Lerrigo. Dr. Mills would see me through the ordeal.

It must have been a long operation. They found this pesky, little, unnecessary wormlike appendage (my appendix) had entwined itself around my cecum. That meant there would have to be a drainage tube to handle any unforeseen infection. Later in my life, when another surgeon saw the huge scar, he remarked that it must have been a long time ago. Sixty-two years is definitely more than a half century.

As I said, I don't know how long the operation took. My problem, however, was coming out of the ether fog. I retched. I had headaches. I was exhausted, and the ether smell seemed to stay with me.

I was afraid I might move and pull out the stitches. And I was told to lie back and not move around too much. Then came a day when I was allowed to turn onto my side. Later, I was allowed to sit up for a spell. Then I could dangle my legs. It was quite different from the way they do surgery these days. In today's hospital, they get you up soon after surgery and make you move around; it's only a short time before you're shedding your johnny and putting on your street clothes. But more than a half century ago, strict bed rest was the rule. The day they finally let me get out of bed and put my feet on the floor, it felt like a thousand needles went through my body.

Eventually I mended and was allowed to leave the hospital—with strict rules about what I could and could not do. There were some positive things. I remember the wonderful back rubs and the tender loving care the white-capped nurses gave me. There were also "probies" from the nursing school whose cheerful help aided my recovery. Those are the only positive things I care to remember about my big "opening."

How different it is today! We have professional, skilled outpatient procedures. And it works. There is none of the prolonged after-effects of old-fashioned anesthesia. All the methods are designed for a quick and successful resolution of whatever ails you.

If surgery today frightens you, you should have experienced it the old-fashioned way. It makes you appreciate the efficiency of today's professionals. I'll take my next "patch up" the modern way, thank you.

OPENING MOVES

I was shopping in one of Bennington's supermarkets the other day when another little old lady sidled up to me. We were in the produce department and she handed me one of the plastic bags they have there. "I just can't get this danged thing open," she said.

I handed her the one I had struggled to open a few seconds earlier. "These old fingers just don't work as well as they used to," I sympathized.

"At my age," she said, "I have a lot of trouble with things like this." She was 89, just two years older than I.

This morning, I took a little box of dried fruit out of my pantry. On the top, in bright letters, it said: "E-Z Open Carton." Not quite! I had to tear the top off in pieces before I could get my fruit treat.

Another day, I tried to open a package of bacon. The "easy instructions" told me simply to "pull apart." Before I was finished, I had to take a pair of pliers and a pair of scissors to the package to get a couple of slices of bacon.

I don't know what I'd do without a pair of pliers and this little red-handled gadget I own to help get the lids off jars. I still have one jar of dill pickles I haven't been able to open. I also want to try some homemade salsa that someone gave me, but even the "homemade" jar resists any of my efforts to remove the top.

I used to buy milk in a carton that has the kind of opening you squeeze to make a funnel. I've given up on that brand; I just couldn't get the squeeze right. I now buy milk in plastic bottles that have a little red strip that you tear off, and a cap that lifts off.

I also have a running feud with my pharmacist. She forgets to put an "adult" cap on my prescription bottle. Those little child-proof caps are also "adult-proof" if you happen to be my age. Of course, even when I get the medicine in an easy-opening bottle, I have another age-related problem: I can't always remember when I took my last pill. Is it time for another pill already?

Cereal boxes are also a chore for some of us. Getting the box open isn't so hard, but the cellophane bag inside is another challenge. It's supposed to pull apart easily, so you can fold it back down and keep the product fresh. But no matter how careful I am about removing the top, I always seem to wind up taking my trusty paring knife to get at my breakfast food. I've decided to get a big plastic container with a screw-off top for my cereal.

The problem doesn't end in the supermarket or kitchen. I can't pump my own gas either. The first time I tried it, I couldn't squeeze the release. In my frustration, I accidentally pulled the nozzle out of the tank and spilled gasoline all over the car and ground. Not wanting to be daunted, I tried again. But I just couldn't get the hang of it. I was thwarted two times in a row. I am not going to try three times. Three times is an "out" in my book. So even though it costs more, I always look for a full service gas station.

Maybe it's just part of getting old. Years ago things really did seem to be easier. I recall how easy it used to be to lift off the little paper top that old-fashioned glass milk bottles had. Underneath that paper wrapping was a little tab that further sealed the milk. Used to be, when we shopped, we put the vegetables and fruits into a paper sack or a market basket; none of those pesky plastic bags. Sliced bacon and other meats used to be sliced to order.

Ground meat came in a little pasteboard tray—without today's impenetrable plastic wrap.

It seems to me the manufacturing world should be kinder to us old folk. There are a lot of us, and it would be nice to be able to move through life without being frustrated with those nitty-gritty lift-offs and sealings that protect our comestibles. Sometimes I think I'm either going to have to find a neighbor who's younger and more dextrous than I. . . .or get myself a new pair of hands.

TOP OF THE LIST

The *National Geographic Travelers* magazine survey was printed in a recent *Banner* and lists the places a well-traveled person should visit in his or her lifetime. And would you believe that Vermont was on the top 50 list?!

It took two years for the *Travelers* magazine to complete this list. As we come to the end of this 20th century it is fitting that the magazine should make these choices.

Now let's go over the list and see if I qualify as a well-traveled person. There are a good many exciting places I have not traveled to. For instance the African Serengeti, the coral reefs of Papua, New Guinea, Antarctica, coastal Norway, Vietnam, Jerusalem, the Amazon forest, Galápagos Islands, Kerala in India, a national park in Chili, Angkor Wat in Cambodia, the Great Wall of China, Machu Picchu in Peru, Petra in Jordan, the Pyramids, and the Taj Mahal.

But I have seen the majestic Alps, Big Sur in California, the Canadian Rockies, the Loire valley in France with those grand chateaux, Australia, New Zealand, Fiji and Samoan islands, Tahiti, Hong Kong, Taiwan, Barcelona, Turkey, Venice (where we rode in a gondola and were serenaded), several of the Greek islands (I'd like to visit more of them), the Hawaiian islands, Thailand, and Vatican City to name a few of the selected must-see places.

In all, I've visited 49 states. Only Alaska remains to be seen. I haven't given up hope that I may get there via a cruise ship.

I have yearned to see the Taj Mahal, that white marble mausoleum built in 1630 by Shah Jahan for his wife in Agra, India. I never really wanted to go to India, though, because I couldn't bear to see all those street people and how the caste system works. I wanted to see the Pyramids, which I likely will never see, and the Serengeti plains, which one of my sons visited and said are unbelievably breathtaking with all the animals.

I did spend five days in Hong Kong, which was necessary to have outfits of brocade and raw silk made to order. I looked across into mainland China; 30 years ago travel into that area was not possible.

In Istanbul I saw the famous Topkapi Palace with all its jewels and the harems of the sultans. I went down in the salt mines in Austria where the Nazis stored the stolen art from all over Europe. A lot of beautiful cathedrals were on my itinerary and there were many other sights around the world I can't recall at the moment. All great memories.

Finally, it is nice to know that I have chosen one of the top 50 places of *National Geographic Travelers* magazine to visit. I not only visited that place—Vermont—but I stayed.

HOT OFF THE PRESS

One day while I was channel surfing to find something of interest on TV, I happened upon a retired man's hobby of printing miniature books. They were works of art and had a large price tag on them. But what interested me was not the artwork so much as the labor that went into printing them. He had California type cases, a little snapper press and all the old-time printing equipment with which I was familiar.

In the 20s, as the daughter of a country newspaper editor, I sat on a high stool, picked up those little pieces of type, put them in a "stick" and set them in a galley ready to be placed in the newspaper forms. I thought it was neat to learn to feed a printing press that had a foot-pedal operation. Eventually my father electrified his old-style presses and we had easier and faster printing equipment.

How clearly all those memories flooded back as I watched this dear old compositor and craftsman produce something of beauty from that old-fashioned out-of-date machinery. It focused the sharp contrast of today's technology in the publishing world.

Recently I needed several copies of an article and took it to a local copy place. When a young man asked if I wanted them collated and stapled I said "yes". We used to call it "assembling". And to hold the pages together we used a stapler with a foot pedal on it.

How do they do that? Technology in the printing industry has advanced so fast in the 70+ years since I "set type". Life in the small Nebraska town moved at a pace that suited the times. Our little berg boasted of a medical doctor, hardware store, three garages, a bank, a drug store with a registered pharmacist, two general stores, two restaurants, two creameries (who today can tell you what they are?), barber shop, meat market with an honest-to-goodness butcher who cut the meat in front of your eyes. There was a rooming house, a grade 1 through 12 school, two churches, a grain elevator, and a telephone exchange with an operator who answered the switchboard around the clock. There were perhaps other businesses I have forgotten, but we were a self-sufficient community. Later my father bought a typesetting machine and I learned to operate it. Away with the little pieces of type that made putting out a paper so laborious! We had advanced our technology 1,000 percent! My father also did bookbinding and as I watched the old hobbyist on TV, I understood part of the art. This old man was doing a labor of love and leaving a legacy to mankind.

At the tender age of 14 I thought I could write a column for the weekly paper. My father, who thought that his children should be seen and not heard, reluctantly printed my first column. It was called "This 'n That" by Abigail. Later when my husband and I published a chain of weekly papers in Kansas I renewed that column using the same "Abigail" identity.

No one wants to go back to those days of such laborious tasks. We just want to recollect them. But it doesn't keep me from taking a nostalgic trip via an old man's hobby. It took a switching of the TV channels to bring me back to the present.

THE LURE OF SPORTS

I'm not sleeping well these days. Something has been robbing me of my sleep. The thief is the late-night NBA playoffs. I'm a sports fan!

I was "hooked" on sports early in life. We lived in a small Midwestern town where the high school had a sports program. The football team had helmets every bit as fancy as the ones at the Football Hall of Fame in Canton, Ohio, it seems. The teams had knee pads and other gear that seemed hardly adequate to dull the jolts of a ferocious tackler. Forward passes and laterals weren't used much in my early days, so it was just plain slogging ahead with the awful bone-crushing tackles sturdy farm boys could give.

The football field was different, too. The downs marker was just two sticks with a chain. A sideline judge called the downs as they were played. I don't know what kind of fancy paint they use today, but in my youth, the football field had lines marked with lime, applied by hand with a bucket and a funnel.

Our basketball gym was a small one. We called it the "cage." Perhaps that's where we get the name "cagers." Girls had a basketball team, and the court was marked in zones. The players had to stay in those zones or they would receive a foul.

Track and field sports were run in what I think used to be a pasture. I think they made the hurdles in the Manual Training shop. Our school had a lively track program with shotput, javelin throw, pole vault, and high jumps, in addition to the races and relays.

It wasn't until many years later, when I moved to North Adams, Massachusetts, that I saw my first hockey game. They had just built a new rink. What I saw I didn't like. I thought it was too rough. Soccer is a sport I have never followed.

We did have tennis, however. We played on a single court behind one of the churches. As I remember them, the racquets were loosely strung and heavy. It was also during the Depression, and there was usually just one ball between the players.

Bowling intrigued me, but I didn't learn how to bowl until I was in my fifties.

I did take golf lessons. I couldn't drive the ball very far and I was not a good putter. It was fun, though, and the exercise was good for me. When I travel, I like to see golf courses. I was in California at Pebble Beach for one of the U.S. West tournaments. I've also looked at courses in Florida, Ohio, and other states. My husband and I wanted to see the Masters' course in Augusta, Georgia, but that course is so shrouded with trees and shrubs we couldn't see a single green.

Professional football and pro basketball remain my favorite spectator sports. I remember attending Celtic games in Boston in the old Garden, and wondering if the old grandstands we sat in would hold up under the weight of the crowds. I've never visited the new Fleet Center. But who knows? I may make that scene yet . . . if the Celtics ever get their act together.

Yes, I'm sports minded. You can have all the soaps, game shows, TV movies, and documentaries you want, but I prefer the action of a good athletic team, even if those NBA playoffs do play hob with my sleeping schedule.

FANCY FOOTWEAR

I noticed the other day that a friend of mine had added heel plates to her shoes. The image made me think about the kind of shoes we wore 80 years ago. We began life by wearing knitted or crocheted booties and we worked our way up to lace-up or high-top side-button shoes. At the beginning of each school year, my father would take us to a big store where we were "shoed" for the coming year. We kept graduating, from high-tops to Mary Janes, to oxfords, to sandals, and to pumps with what used to be called a military heel. Finally we would get our first pair of high heels.

In my youth, some shoe repairs were done at home. We had a shoe last in our house. A last is a metal form in the shape of a foot. I recall watching my father make temporary repairs on it if a tack or nail worked through the sole. If more serious repairs were called for, we took the shoes to the shoemaker, whose skill would ensure that you'd be wearing those oxfords or high-tops for many more months. When I was growing up, we didn't have a lot of shoes to choose from; not even a second pair for Sunday best. We made things last longer.

One of the repairs the shoemaker used to make was to do half soles, heels, or add heel plates to the shoes. Not only did the plates make the shoes last longer, they also made a little click-clack as we walked. As a young girl, I liked the sound.

I remember the time I got my first spike heels. It was my last year in high school and I'd saved enough to buy spikes. Nylons were not being made yet, so I put on black silk stockings. If I didn't look like a specimen with my storky legs! I think I must have looked like youngsters who dress up in their mother's clothes. Walking in spikes was also a learning experience.

Today, the favored shoe seems to be sneakers. It took quite a bit of courage for me to buy my first pair of "tennies." I thought old ladies looked weird and a bit too youthful in them. But one pair convinced me that comfort was important and appearance be damned. Sneakers, slides, and sandals are just more comfortable.

I still have dress shoes for Sundays and other festive occasions, but as soon as I get home, they come right off. My shoe size has increased over the years, from 7 1/2 AAA to 9A. But no matter what the size, I like my sneakers. I put them on and I'm ready to begin my day.

DIAPER GENIES AND OTHER INVENTIONS

A few weeks ago I went down Boston way to meet my first step great-grandson. It was not only a pleasing experience, it was an eye-opener. So much has happened in what I call the "baby world." Even parenting has changed.

My visit to the nursery began the revelation. Sixty years ago, when I became a mother, I thought I was very modern to have a crib whose side would drop down with the touch of a foot lever. In my step great-grandsons's nursery, the crib itself would adjust to different levels. The design allowed it to become a child's bed, and later to become a twin bed. At the head of the crib there was a monitor so sensitive the baby's breathing could be heard in the next room.

Next to the changing table was a warming device for the baby wipes. What really made my eyes bulge was the Diaper Genie™. What a gadget! You place the soiled Pamper™ in a little barrel-like cannister, turn a crank, and presto, the diaper is sealed and shoved into a container. When emptied the contents look like a roll of sausages. No mess. No fuss. No smell!

In the feeding department, today's parents have an appliance that holds a frozen block for keeping the formula cold. No more trips downstairs in the middle of the night to get a bottle for baby. The same appliance also has a heating unit to bring the formula up to feeding temperature.

When I had my children, playpens were essentially a wood

cage around a mattress, which sat on the floor. Today's playpens are at a height so you don't have to stoop to put the baby in it. There's a swing apparatus with a timer on it, so you don't ever have to rock the baby to sleep. A little day seat has a comforting vibrator mechanism in it. The high chair is one that the youngster will be able to use for many years. It has a tray big enough for a four-course meal.

I think back to when my children were babies. We had birds-eye cloth diapers (no Pampers™). They had to be laundered; we couldn't just throw them away. They always made the baby look very round in the lower region, where the diaper was bunched for absorption. We put belly bands on new infants and pinned them with tiny safety pins. Big safety pins held the diapers in place.

Usually the layette consisted of kimonos with a drawstring at the bottom, and little sacks for body warmth and little underslips. Shirts had strings to close them. There were soft booties. Today, there are no strings, hooks and eyes, buttons or pins; only Velcro™ and snaps that make it easy to dress a wiggly infant. Clothing styles are also different. My new step great-grandson has blue jeans with a tiny one-inch zipper to provide easy access to the diaper underneath.

For my first child, a friend loaned us a wicker baby carriage. I rather liked the English-style pram, but today's infant is wheeled around in a stroller that is collapsible and easily carried in the car.

When I was a mother, we held our babies when we rode in the car. Nowadays they are protected in specially designed carriers in the back seat. I think it's strange how soon a fussy infant stops crying when the car motor starts.

What's also nice is that my step granddaughter is so happy with this phase of her life that she has opted to stay home and give up her career as an executive. I wish it were possible for all mothers to have that option.

GRANDMA'S SPECIAL DAY

Her name was Bessie. Bessie had senile dementia and lived in a nursing home. She was a sweet grandma, gracious and loving. But the past seemed to have been locked out of her memory for many years. When it came time for her granddaughter's wedding, a special effort was made to make it a pleasant memory—however fleeting—for her.

She was dressed in a pale pink frock complete with matching accessories. One of the nurses gave her a manicure. Her hair had been shampooed and set and later given a fluff-up before she left the facility. A bit of blush was applied to grandma's cheeks, and they did her lips for her. White shoes, not worn for many years, were found in a closet, and grandma got some support hose to make sure her stockings wouldn't droop.

The nursing home personnel saw she was ready on time to be checked out of the facility for the afternoon. As she left the nursing home, she moved cautiously with a certain grace, almost as if she were the bride. She knew how good she looked, as if she were a queen. As she passed the admiring nursing staff, they told her how pretty she was. Several even planted a kiss on her blooming cheeks.

My husband and I would be her chauffeurs to the wedding. Bessie knew it was a special day. She had at least the glimmer of an idea that her granddaughter, Sara Jane, was getting married.

Surprisingly, when Bessie arrived at the church, she recognized a few people and even called them by name. She looked at one of the groomsmen—her grandson—and called him by name. He answered with the family's pet name for Bessie: "Mom mom." He told her how lovely she looked.

The mother of the bride asked Bessie if she had her hanky.

"What for?" asked Bessie.

"Everyone cries at weddings," the mother answered.

But Bessie sat dry-eyed through the entire ceremony. In a vague way, perhaps she was trying to recall scenes and memories of the past that weren't coming into clear focus. It was an effort. When the bride floated by in a state of ecstasy, Bessie murmured, "What a lovely bride. She looks just like Sara Jane."

Going through the receiving line was trying for Bessie. Faint recollections came and went briefly. On one occasion she remembered that one friend's wife had died and recalled her name.

After the reception, it was time for Bessie to return to the nursing home. She was ready to go. She kept repeating that it had been a wonderful day, but oh how glad she would be to kick off her shoes and lie down and rest.

It was a big event for Bessie, one that might return in flashes of memory and recognition. The family would remember the times when their grandma (their "mom mom") was a whole person. But on this one, bright June day, she was a member of the wedding.

THE GENERAL STORE

When I opened a box of store-bought cookies the other day it set me to thinking how "boughten" cookies were dispensed years ago.

We had two general stores in my little town. The cookies were displayed in a tier of square, glass-covered boxes and were sold by the pound. Not all the cookies were the same size or weight, and sometimes the clerk had to experiment before he figured out how many were in a pound.

Of course, the store-bought cookies were never as good as the homemade ones, but the choices were larger. The kind of cookies were similar to those available today. There were Fig Newtons™, big round sugar cookies, raisin-oatmeal, crisp sugar wafers, and chocolate-covered puffs that had squishy marshmallow inside. Those were just a few of our choices. The store also had jelly beans in a large wooden bucket. You could buy a couple of pennies' worth and satisfy your sweet tooth.

Candy and cookies weren't the only things available. When you bought bacon, your order was filled by the butcher who sliced off the amount and thickness you wanted. "He sometimes weighed his thumb" is an old cliche that was often true.

Hamburger was ground to order—none of that nice-looking red stuff that you see already prepackaged and who knows what's in it. None of those hermetically sealed plastic wrap meats that you need scissors or a sharp knife to open.

Eggs came from a large double square crate brought in from the farm. Most of the time they were candled in the store; they were held up to a light to make sure they hadn't already begun to be chicken embryos.

We grew most of our own vegetables at home. They either came right out of the garden or from the cellar where they had been canned and stored the season before. Fresh lettuce and greens from the garden were so different from the wilted varieties we find prepackaged today. Potatoes came from the cellar, sometimes with a bit of soil left on them from when they were stored in the fall. Potatoes lasted all winter long. Apples were stored in a barrel kept in the cellar.

We didn't often buy bread in the store either. Bread was always baked at home. Oh, how the smell of freshly baked loaves still lingers! We bought flour in 50- or 100-pound cloth bags. The cloth became tea towels later on. It wasn't unusual, either, to buy sugar in a 100-pound bag.

We used Morton's™ salt in our home. I remember the little girl logo on the outside of the carton carrying an umbrella in the rain as the salt spilled out the bottom of her bag. That logo is still used by Morton's, but in a much smaller size.

The general store sold piece goods, rickrack, lace, yarn, needles, bias tape, thread, and other notions for dressmaking at home. In the Nebraska town where I lived there was an old maid clerk who measured off the piece goods and managed the dry goods department.

Nowadays everything is so different. No more one-stop shopping. Are there still stores like that? I mean general stores where you can pick up food, clothing needs, harness, hardware, and sundries. Our little town was self-sustaining and we did not have to go to a larger town to shop.

Those were the good old days.

Just the Facts . . . . or All the Details

After reading about weddings in the *Banner* and seeing how little was said about such a big event in the lives of young marrieds (and sometimes oldsters), I was amused when I picked up a small-town Kansas weekly paper and read the glowing report of a local wedding. I just have to share this!

The tapers were lighted by two young men attired in Ascot gray tuxedos with white pleated shirts with cummerbunds and bow ties. The groom was attired in an Ascot gray Lexington tuxedo with a white pleated shirt, gray vest and bow tie. The best man wore an Ascot gray Devon tuxedo. [They didn't say what kind of shorts they wore.]

The maid of honor wore a ballerina length dress of candlelight ivory satin with a delicate floral imprint. Her hair was held by an ivory satin floral hairpiece and her bouquet was a miniature of the bride's. The flower girl's dress was similar to that of the maid of honor; she wore a shirred ivory lace head band and an ivory carnation wristlet. She carried a natural ivory wicker basket accented with a red and green plaid bow from which she dropped sprigs of holly.

The bride entered the sanctuary wearing a ballerina length dress of candlelight ivory satin, overlaid with ivory Rachel lace. It featured a bandeau neckline accented at the shoulders with tiny satin ribbons, 3/4 length shirred lace sleeves and a dropped basque waistline. The fitted bodice was accented with seed pearls and iridescent sequins. The back was cut in a deep V from which fell tiny satin bows to the waistline. Ivory lace gauntlets and ivory pearl accessories accented her dress. She wore a large brimmed hat of reembroidered lace accented with an apple blush rose. The chapel length veil fell from a net poof. She carried a bouquet of ivory silk poinsettias nestled in a cluster of holly. The bride designed the bouquets.

And so went the glowing and extensive report of the wedding. A reception was held with the three-tiered cake baked by a friend; each tier was a combination of chocolate and white cake, symbolizing the uniting of the couple's lives. A buffet of strawberry slush, mulled cider, and coffee was served. The couple's toast was made using German crystal goblets, a gift from the groom's brother from Germany. After the wedding, parchment scrolls and wheat bags (what else in Kansas!) were passed out.

I thought about all those minute details and assumed that in the Midwest this is the way weddings were reported. I was brought up short later when I found a clipping of my wedding printed in a Kansas weekly 63 years ago. My gawd! I didn't even recognize the person they were describing. I do know that it was in the dead of winter, a time of depression when it was necessary for my parents to supply coal to heat the church for our afternoon wedding.

There were so many details to report that it took a whole column to relate that an almost old maid had made it to the altar. They reported everything, even the fact that my father had an ingrown toenail and wore an open-toe shoe when he gave me away.

What a difference in reporting in that small Kansas newspaper (not my father's) and a daily paper such as the *Banner*. I guess small-town readers are interested in every detail. I wonder if city brides like to have all the descriptions a matter of public record. I think they would prefer to have "just the facts, ma'am."

A PENNY FOR YOUR THOUGHTS

The first government one-cent postcard was issued May 1, 1873. It was a cheap—but not fast—way to send a message or announcement. Today's postcards cost 20 times as much. But it's not just the cost. Everything costs more these days. I liked those penny postcards. My mother wrote very small and could get a whole letter onto a card. Years later, when I left the nest, I looked forward to those postcards.

We can't send postcards for a penny anymore, but some of those postcards are still around. My son found a penny postcard in some old family memorabilia. He framed it along with this column and sent it to the North Bennington post office, where they said they would exhibit it on one of the walls. They did!

Every once in a while I get the urge to see what I have tucked away in my desk. I didn't find any penny postcards, but I did discover some four-cent cards, and some six- and eight-cent ones.

I sometimes add the extra postage and send them out. I've always been a postcard writer. One of my joys has been to send picture postcards from places I visit. Even when I didn't get them posted in the place I was visiting, I kept them as a reminder of where I'd been. I have a little cache of them.

I also want to talk about stamps. Have you been to the post office lately and seen the beautiful stamps available? They display gorgeous flowers, fruits, berries, Walt Disney characters, historical personages, the national emblem, Uncle Sam, and aquatic scenes.

There are commemorative stamps that remind us of past events and famous people.

The government Post Office is really revving up the artistry of stamps and they are eye-catching. From my point of view, the most important change is that you don't have to lick stamps anymore. Today's self-sticking stamps come with their own adhesive in convenient little books, sheets, and rolls.

President Franklin Roosevelt was a philatelist. I believe his huge collection is on display in his library in Hyde Park, New York. My older son once aspired to be a stamp collector. He started a stamp collection over 55 years ago, thinking that they would grow in value and he could cash in on them when he went to college. That didn't happen. There's more to collecting stamps than buying pretty pictures. I think he still has the collection somewhere.

While I'm in this postal mood, I want to say that the most accommodating crew of government employees I've ever encountered is right here in the North Bennington post office. They are always courteous, accommodating, and eager to give advice about any mailing service. They even share local information and are never too hurried to pass the time of day.

Our little post office was recently renovated. The force endured the clutter and inconvenience without sacrificing their goodwill. Now we have a very neat postal delivery place with lots of lockboxes. It's surprising to me how many people still like to go to the post office for their mail.

PRACTICE, PRACTICE, PRACTICE

The recital at Park-McCullough mansion this month by pianist Elizabeth Kim left me marveling at her keyboard skill. I know even the best of pianists spend a lot of time practicing.

When I was six, my mother thought I should learn to play the piano. I was taken to Grace Fike, our local music teacher. She had one leg shorter than the other and wore a built-up shoe. I recall that she was a very gentle woman and gave lessons in her home.

I remember my first lesson. It cost a quarter for an hour of instruction. Miss Fike had me hold my wrists up straight, so she could balance a pencil on them. I was then taught the keys, and innumerable finger exercises and scales. I did my practice faithfully as it sometimes got me out of household tasks such as dusting and wiping dishes, which I disdained.

I don't recall how long I was a pupil of Miss Fike's. We moved to another state. Once again I took lessons. The new teacher gave lessons in her sister's home. She had an invalid mother at her house, and a stream of young pupils and the noise of missed notes was too much for the mother.

But what a beautiful teacher she was. She began where I left off with Miss Fike and started me on a series of graded books. I had a little orange exercise book (I think I still have it somewhere), and my 100s were pleasing to my mother. However, one day I hadn't practiced enough and my grade on one piece plummeted to 98. I returned home, vowing I would never take any more lessons. I was a failure!

Fortunately, I continued and went through four graded books. I wish I could remember the name of them. Finally I felt I no longer wanted to take lessons. I was becoming a helper to my father on his newspaper and that seemed to take priority.

That was the end of my piano playing, even though I occasionally sat down and picked out some old pieces. I liked to play sheet music. The songs I played back then included "Barney Google", "Ain't She Sweet?", "Who's Sorry Now?" and "Doodly Do."

When I went to hear Miss Kim, I saw a pianist I'm sure never digressed from her desire to be a great musician. Her ability made me wonder at the marvelous sounds that came forth from the black and whites.

Alas for me. After all those years, I cannot play a tune. Even reading music is a chore. It just goes to show that "practice makes perfect" and my defection from that has made me a piano illiterate. I wish I had worked more at it.

My first son began lessons at an early age. I'd hoped he would become a virtuoso. But practice was not his bag, even though I insisted that he continue his lessons. One day his teacher called and said she had an "unhappy little fellow sitting on her porch steps because [she] refused to give him his lesson and take his dollar." He had not done his practicing.

That was an incentive that later made him work at practicing. He did appear in a recital and was very proud of the dollar he was paid. To this day he can still play that recital piece. Now he composes music and knows more about music than I ever thought possible. He can't make a living at piano work—he didn't practice that much. But it just shows you can accomplish a goal.

CABBAGE NIGHTS OF OLD

'T is the season of Halloween. I expect to have a few goblins, Supermen, Batmen, pumpkin bodies, and princesses come to my door and I hope they arrive early. And I hope enough come so that I won't be left with any of those candy bars to eat.

I don't remember trick-or-treating as a child. We just weren't allowed to go out. Nor did we have any costumes. It was just something we didn't know too much about. I learned about it later, when I had children of my own.

I do know about "Cabbage Night," though. "Cabbage Night" was the night before Halloween. I don't advise any youngsters to do what the town clowns and cutups did back then, although I do laugh as I look back.

We were in our first year of marriage and living in a small town in Kansas. I had never heard of Cabbage Night. But I remember going out to the main drag the next morning to see what had taken place the night before.

There were still a few buggies in our little berg. Lo and behold! On top of some of the tin awnings over the storefronts were buggies, farm equipment, corn stalks, old inner tubes, and signs taken from gas stations. Outhouses (we had a lot of those, not having any waterworks for our village) had been tipped over. One outhouse—it happened to be ours—was taken blocks away and left on Main Street. Everybody thought it was a huge joke on the young married couple. In a way, it was a good thing. The loss of our outhouse prompted us to get a new Chick Sales unit; Chick Sales units were government-issue privies.

I never had so many chuckles as I did the morning after Cabbage Night. I couldn't believe in that quiet little town the mischief makers could accomplish all they did without arousing the townspeople. The next day there were many hands who were willing to take the buggies off the awnings and put Main Street back in order.

It saddens me, though, that some people destroy the spirit of Halloween by putting razor blades, needles, pins, and sharp pieces of glass in their treats. Some parents I know wouldn't allow their children to go out alone to trick-or-treat so they went along to make sure their children were safe. I want to make sure my place is a "safe house" for those young goblins and superheroes. We should all do the same.

NICE TO REMEMBER, NOT TO GO BACK

"I'm tired of hearing about all that happens to you when you grow older," one of the over-60 ladies in our church circle complained. The group had exhausted—or so they thought—all the information and pitfalls of aging in previous programs. They had had enough.

Our ingenious program chairman turned the table on members of our circle. She offered a program called "Nostalgia, or The Good Old Days." Our ladies tackled the topic with vigor. Not only did we list the good times, we rated them as plus or minus. Here are some of our findings.

Lower prices! What a revelation that was. We had ladies who could remember a loaf of bread for a dime. Movies were 15 cents. Gasoline was 15 cents a gallon. There were lower rents and lower prices for clothing and for the fabric we bought to make our own clothes. One wit reminded us, though, that those lower prices were accompanied by terribly low wages.

Our circle discussed pollution and bemoaned what is happening today. They also observed that the plastic cups, paper plates, napkins, and paper tablecloths used for our luncheon might be a contributing factor.

"What about all the waste and bulging landfills, overflowing dumpsters, and general litter?" we asked. One woman observed that disposable diapers account for so much waste today. We laughed at that one. We could all remember the days when we had to wash diapers. None of us wanted to do that again.

The group felt there were fewer divorces in the good old days. One of the women, however, reminded us that even then all marriages weren't good and happy. Women were homemakers who often didn't have the choice or means to get out of an unhappy situation.

There were fewer cars then. Somehow we all managed to get to shopping areas, grocery stores and the church. We walked. Children walked to neighborhood schools, or they shared rides with neighbors. Today it is more cars, fewer people in each car, more pollution, and bumper-to-bumper traffic.

The women remembered neighborliness as a plus. We used to be able to go next door for a cup of sugar or a bit of flour to finish up a recipe. If there was sickness, death, or a crisis, neighbors were the first to offer support.

Years ago families sat down to eat meals together. Now dinners are prepared for whomever happens to be home at the odd hour. We are so busy. Meals are eaten from a TV tray in front of the television. There's little opportunity to discuss family topics, projects, or even to share our stories of the day.

Medicine has changed. Nowadays we have to get our aging bodies to the doctor's office or emergency room. Many of us remembered how the doctors used to make house calls. We talked about cholesterol. We talked about the advantages and disadvantages of intergenerational living in the same home.

When the time came to adjourn, our group kept going. We didn't want to go back to those "good old days." But we did want to remember them and we enjoyed making comparisons with what we elders see as today's world.

MEAN GREEN PARTY MACHINE

You think balloons are just for kids? Put that thought out of your mind and read this tale. It's about the waltzing Mylar™ balloons and an 80th birthday.

It was my husband's 80th birthday, and—by choice—he didn't want gifts. Just a cake and a card signed by all present. But the family did present him with a large box. "It's a funsy," they said. It didn't weigh very much, but it was a big box. When he opened the top, he jumped back. A number of decorated Mylar™ balloons flew out. Each balloon had a pertinent message. I especially remember the one that said "Mean Green Party Machine."

When it came time to go home, we put the balloons into the car trunk. I thought they might deflate before we returned to our apartment. Not so! They were alive and active and ready to make themselves at home. For three weeks they were never still. Air currents caused "Mean Green Party Machine" and "Happy Birthday" to play strange games. They began to float around and they would come into our bedroom. They would move into the living room. They whipped around the corner into the den. They even floated right into the kitchen. One hovered over a chair like a child expecting to be fed and one ended up piggyback on an oscillating fan.

I'm a light sleeper and frequently get up at night. It was a strange sensation to encounter those activated Mylar™ creations. They were never at rest. Sometimes they would hover together. I noticed one night the streetlights reflected on their shiny surfaces and it gave them an eerie appearance. If I hadn't known what they were, they would have frightened me. One night I woke up and "Mean Green Party Machine" was wafting over my sleeping husband. It seemed they wanted to be friendly, day and night.

After one particularly hot night, one of the balloons pressed against the window screen as if to say "Yeee-ow! It sure is hot in this room." Another morning, one of the balloons waited at the apartment door, almost as if it wanted to go out and see the big wide world.

One of the little imps kept floating over to the breakfast table chair. Another hovered over the 80-year-old's easy chair, as if to entice him to pay attention to it. "Mean Green Party Machine" was the most aggressive. He would quiver on the sofa as if to say "Come and sit with me." A fourth balloon had given up its ghostly flights and was inanimate in an easy chair.

Three of the balloons never lost their buoyancy. Just when we thought they were about to "expire," another draft would come and they would whip out of a corner where they were resting and go on the move again.

Those colorful, animated, armless, headless bags of noncombustible gas had more energy than the grandchildren. None of our grandchildren ever floated to the ceiling.

The Mylar™ (polyethylene teraphthalate) from which the balloons were made is a product of the DuPont Company in Delaware. Some entrepreneur converted this strong, gossamer aluminized plastic into balloons that celebrate many occasions: birthdays, graduations, weddings, retirements—you name it.

Balloons aren't just for kids. They're for grown-ups too. So if life ever gets boring for you older folks, buy a bunch of Mylar™ "balloons, turn on the fan or air-conditioner, take a seat in your easy chair, and watch the show. These creations are charmers and great entertainers.

South Bend Malleable

Winter is coming on now, and it gets me thinking about how my family used to heat our homes and do our cooking. The star of the show for us was our old kitchen range.

Ours had six lids (for cooking) and an attached reservoir where water was poured in and kept hot for washing dishes. There was a warming oven above the burners. Two of the six lids had three circular plates. If we wanted to cook with a small pan, we took off the inner plate; if we had a big pan, we took off all three of the plates. There was a little plate lifter that came in various designs. Ours had a wire loop for a handle.

On one side of the range there was a lift-up lid where we put wood or coal into the grate. Sometimes we even used corn cobs. We had lots of cobs in Iowa and they burned with intense but not lasting heat.

What always amazed me was how my mother could make homemade bread and always have it come out so nicely browned. There was a thermometer on the oven door, but I never understood how it got to the proper temperature.

There were some nice adornments on that old stove, like a steel decorative piece on the warming oven and oven door. The text proclaimed proudly that this was a "South Bend Malleable." Obviously it was manufactured in Indiana where there were many forges.

Special utensils were required for the old ranges. For example, we had a three-legged iron kettle that fit directly over the heat and was used for making soup. Cooking was done in heavy cast-iron skillets and granite pots and pans; aluminum was not available then.

We had a wire contraption for holding bread as we toasted it over the stove top. Sometimes we got in a hurry and tried to make toast by lifting the lids and putting the bread directly above the flame. Burnt toast!

Coming home after playing in the snow, mittens were dried in the oven and when the oven wasn't needed for baking bread, we left the door ajar for added heat in the room. On cold mornings we were permitted to dress in front of the open oven.

That old range had to be polished and blackened occasionally to keep it looking good. There was a wood box near the stove and it was our chore to keep it filled. I learned about "lazy man's load" when I tried to carry in more chunks than I could handle, and dropped some on my toes.

Under the oven was a little compartment where soot accumulated. It had to be cleaned out with a flat rake. The stovepipes had to be taken down and the soot removed from them. That was usually a Spring job. The old collars that fit around the stovepipe where it went into the chimney were often shiny, ornamental rings.

Ashes had to be lifted out of the grate with a small metal shovel. The grate was under only two of the lids and the heat spread across the range top to provide medium, slow, and simmer temperatures.

We used to visit a relative's home in Nantucket where the kitchen's focal point was a handsome kitchen range. It didn't have a warming oven, but it did have little swing-away holders that could be placed over the heat. It had been restored to pristine beauty and was used for a while. Later the family installed a gas-fired unit to heat the kitchen.

But I suppose there are still places in the world where the kitchen range is still used to heat the room. Ours was a utilitarian appliance that made our kitchen a cozy spot on the cold winter days of my childhood.

WHEN TRAINS WERE KING

The Vermont Valley Flyer pulled into our North Bennington station September 25 with Representative Richard Pembroke and his grandson standing on the side of the diesel engine. He spoke to the excited crowd that had gathered to celebrate the inaugural run. For the moment, the train was only an excursion to Manchester, Vermont, but one day the train would go all the way from our little Vermont town right into New York City.

The people waited patiently as the diesel backed up and pushed the coaches into the station siding. Inside the depot, a refreshment table was set up. The North Bennington depot is a handsome Victorian structure recently restored with a gift from Babs McCullough and Bill Scott. A bronze plaque on the side of the building honors their generous gift.

Seeing the excitement and joy took me back to the days when trains were our most used method of transportation. One of my first train trips was in a caboose. Yes, a caboose. This was the "passenger" service from our rural Nebraska town to the county seat. It wasn't elegant or comfortable, but it took us the 12 miles to the bigger town to transact business. We sat along the side of the caboose on benches.

I yearned to go up into the little cabin on top of the caboose. That was where the flagman looked up the tracks to the engineer as they communicated by signals, flags, and lanterns. I never made it up there, but I did look out the rear platform and saw the many ties it took to lay down that iron track. I'm not sure what line it was; it could have been the Missouri Pacific or the Burlington CB&Q (Chicago, Burlington, and Quincy) line.

In World War II, with gas rationing, a lot of long trips were by train. I remember a trip to Little Rock, Arkansas to see my husband; he was in basic training there. I made the entire trip seated on my suitcase in the vestibule. There were no seats available by the time I got on in Kansas City. There were a lot of wives and parents on that trip, and we shared our fears and hopes as we clickety-clacked toward Little Rock.

The dining car was overflowing and couldn't handle the crowd. Vendors who boarded the train at various stations couldn't begin to supply the passengers' needs. When I arrived in Little Rock I was starved. The only nourishment I had was a cookie that some generous person had tucked in her tote.

I remember another big trip. It was 50 years ago, and I was on my way to Los Angeles to be with my mother. She was dying, and I wanted to spend some precious last days with her. I took my two sons with me. We rode in what were called Happy Valley seats. They reclined so we could sleep comfortably. My two boys still remember the two-and-a-half-day trip.

This time, the dining car was prepared. There was real linen on the table. Really delicious food was served three times a day. My boys waited eagerly for the porter to pass through the train, playing the four-note gong that announced the diner was ready to serve. It was exciting to walk the length of the train and find a table that always had a single rose in a vase. The waiters were friendly, efficient, and served the food with a flourish.

Many years later, my husband and I trained from Washington, D.C., to Pinehurst, North Carolina. What a difference! There was no nicely appointed dining car. Only a snack bar and a fast-food buffet.

It would be wonderful if American trains could be as convenient and functional as those in Europe and Japan. They are fast, clean, well maintained, and make traveling easy.

Our little excursion from North Bennington to Manchester brought back those fond memories. Riding the rails on the Valley Flyer will never compare to the great trains of America's past, but for the nonce, I'll always keep pleasant thoughts of the way it used to be.

LOVE OF FLYING

Plane crashes in the news this week stir memories of my first trip off the ground. It was in the 1930s and my husband and I were at a Kansas newspaper convention in Wichita.

The factory that had begun to manufacture jet planes offered editors the opportunity for a flight over the city. Flying was new back then, and some of the editors deferred. Not us! We were eager to go. We climbed aboard and buckled our seat belts. The thrill of rising above the ground and looking down at a miniature city was exciting and exhilarating. I was hooked! That was the way to go.

Shortly after we began our newspaper careers, an area pilot was so despondent over his wife's death that he crashed his plane. He took off and flew a short distance before he nose-dived into a pasture and died instantly. News spread and townspeople gathered at the scene. My husband rushed there with his brownie box camera. He had a big scoop and we were soon on the way to Topeka to leave the film and story with his byline at the *Daily Capital*. I still have an enlargement of that picture. It shows me standing on the edge of the crowd. It's faded and brown now, but it was a big event in our young lives.

We had another flyer in our little town. He was a local merchant who owned a biplane and often flew over the area. My husband went up with him several times as there was room in the cockpit for two. This man had a son who was a polio victim and a nephew who was his son's companion. These young men often visited us and talked about flying. The nephew was Danny Forbes, who became a pilot in World War II and was killed in combat. The air force training base in Topeka was named after Danny.

I also recall my most memorable night flight. We had gone to Europe by ship, and this was my first foreign flight. It was from Paris to Madrid in the 1960s. How wonderful it was to look down in the twilight at the miniature scene below. The takeoff and landing were smooth and added to the thrill. They even served a decent little meal on heavy ceramic dishes. I purchased several of these at a sale later, and still use them for mini-portions.

I take great pleasure in flying. But not always. There was one rough flight I will never forget, from St. Louis to Buffalo. I didn't panic, but I pulled my seat belt a little tighter and thought that if it was my time to go, so be it.

I still fly whenever I have to travel long distances. It isn't quite as easy for oldsters. The airports are huge and plane changes aren't always simple. But I simply ask for a wheelchair, and don't worry about it. I love flying.

The Nakedness of Trees

I look out the window at the little forest around my place and I am sad. The leaves have left their home on the branches of the trees. I know winter is on its way. I love it when my trees are green, even though that means the big trees block the sunlight that would help the little trees grow.

Now, when I walk through my woods, I hear the rustle of the leaves, smell the damp earth after a rain, and feel the sadness that we must face as winter approaches. It's almost as if the trees blush at their nakedness.

When we lived in Delaware, my husband and I used to drive elderly people to doctor's appointments. One of the little old ladies told us that she loved to look at the trees after they lost their leaves. At first, I thought she was getting senile. I'd never thought of naked trees in that respect. Then, I began to stop and look, and became aware of how artistic and intricate the limbs are, particularly of older trees. One lovely white birch stands across the road from me, and I know now that the little old lady we drove wasn't senile. That birch is a winter work of art.

If only we could think of our own lives and souls like those barren trees! We know that trees have their cycles. They must pass into oblivion, just like the days of the week and months of the year. It is a time of quiescence. With trees, we wait for new growth as the seasons roll around.

Alas, it's not that way with us humans. We can't renew these scrawny arms or legs. There are spots on our heads where the hair is no longer lush. There is no season for our bodies to put new spring in our steps. We use clothes to hide the flaws of our aging bodies, as leaves hide the gnarly forks and branches of a tree.

As I look at the naked trees, I wish I had the ability to renew my body like the trees sprout new leaves. I know that's not possible, so I've learned to content myself with the increase of knowledge that we all store in our noggins over the decades. This is our season of growth. This is the way we can be renewed, with thoughts of happy times and events. The human season is quite different from that of trees. It's still a blessing.